DISCOVERING LANGUAGES
LATIN

Elaine S. Robbins

Formerly Mount Logan Middle School
Logan, Utah

Kathryn R. Ashworth

Brigham Young University

AMSCO

When ordering this book, please specify R 595 S
or DISCOVERING LANGUAGES: LATIN

AMSCO SCHOOL PUBLICATIONS, INC.
315 Hudson Street / New York, N.Y. 10013

To the memory of

Carl C. Robbins Jr., beloved son and brother of the authors

Design and Production: Boultinghouse & Boultinghouse, Inc.

Cover Illustration: Delana Bettoli

Illustrations: Delana Bettoli, Rick Brown, Maxie Chambliss, Ric Del Rossi, John R. Jones, Ed Taber

ISBN 0-87720-563-9

To the Student

You are about to embark on a journey of discovery — beginning to learn a new language spoken by millions of people a long time ago, LATIN.

Even though you cannot go to any country to practice Latin, you can still enjoy it and learn a great deal from it. Much of the history of the Western world began in the Latin-speaking world of the Roman Empire. By learning Latin, you will better understand the beginnings of your culture, your cultural roots.

More than half of all English words come from Latin. By learning Latin vocabulary, you will understand and master a great number of English words in a short time. And if you choose to learn a Romance language, such as Spanish, French, or Italian, Latin will be a great help since Romance languages come from Latin.

Latin may be one of several languages you will discover in this course. You can then select which language you will continue to study. Whatever your goals, this book will be a fun beginning in exploring a special gift you have as a human being: the ability to speak a language other than your own.

In this book, you will discover the Latin language and the world where it was spoken. The Latin words and expressions you will learn have been limited so that you will feel at ease.

You will learn how to express many things in Latin: how to greet people, how to count, how to tell the day and month of the year, how to identify and describe many animals and objects, and more.

You will use Latin to talk about yourself and your friends. You will practice with many different activities, like puzzles, word games, cartoons, and pictures. Some activities you will do with classmates or with the whole class. You will act out fun skits and conversations. You will learn about many interesting bits of Latin culture: Romans as builders, Roman baths, Roman life and work, education, toys and games, sports, food, and fashion.

You will also meet young Claudia, who will be your guide on how to pronounce Latin words. Look for Claudia's clues throughout this book and get a feel for the Latin language and its sounds. You will also develop an ear for Latin, so listen carefully to your teacher.

You will quickly realize that learning a new language is not as hard as you might have imagined. Enjoy using it with your teacher and classmates. Try not to be shy or afraid of making mistakes when speaking: remember, the more you speak, the more you will learn. And you can even show off the Latin you learn to family, relatives, and friends.

Now — on to Latin. **Fortuna felicitas!,** which means *Good luck!*

— *K.R.A.*

Contents

Rome and the Latin Language

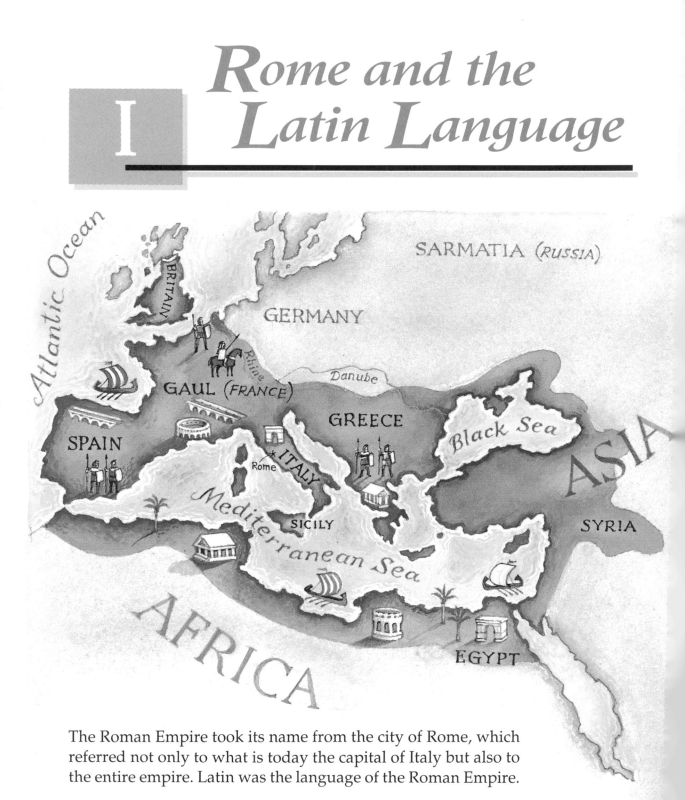

The Roman Empire took its name from the city of Rome, which referred not only to what is today the capital of Italy but also to the entire empire. Latin was the language of the Roman Empire.

According to a legend, Rome was founded about 750 B.C. by Romulus. Historically, Rome began on the east bank of the Tiber River as a farming community. The Tiber divided the Italic people (who would become Romans) from the Etruscans (an important earlier civilization). Around 500 B.C., the Romans overthrew the Etruscans and for four hundred years lived in the Roman Republic. This republic fought many wars with surrounding peoples and eventually conquered parts of modern-day Europe, Africa, and Asia. Of all these invaded countries, Greece had by far the greatest influence on Roman thought, literature, and language.

In the first century B.C., Julius Caesar, Rome's most famous general, conquered Gaul and invaded Germany and England. Rome had become the dominant power in the world and Julius Caesar its most powerful leader. After Caesar's assassination in 44 B.C., his grand-nephew and adopted son, Gaius Octavius, became Rome's first emperor with the title Augustus. He rebuilt cities, reorganized the army, and sponsored the arts and letters. His reign began the three hundred years of peace in the Roman Empire known as **Pax Romana** — the Roman Peace. During this span of time, the Romans built a massive system of roads throughout their empire, some of which exist to this day. They also traded goods by sea.

Altogether, Rome had over fifty emperors. Some of them were famous and achieved great things for Rome. Others are remembered for their tyranny and cruelty. Nero not only "fiddled while Rome burnt" but also persecuted the early Christians. Titus's armies destroyed the holy city of Jerusalem. By 313, the Romans had become more tolerant toward Christianity. Constantine, the first Christian emperor, shifted the seat of power from Rome to Byzantium. He renamed the city Constantinople after himself. Today that city is named Istanbul. In 395, the empire was divided between East and West. Rome, in the Western part, lost most of its power and importance. By 476, the last emperor had lost his empire to the Goths, an invading tribe from the north.

As Roman civilization died, so did its language. Still, through the Middle Ages, Latin continued to function as an official language and flourished in the universities. All educated people spoke Latin in addition to their native language. Today, Latin is called a dead language. No one speaks Latin as a native language, although it is still the official language of the Catholic Church.

If you visit Rome today, you can still see the old Roman Forum or the Colosseum, but they are no longer used for meetings or games. Just as old Roman ruins have lasted to the present and can teach us much, so Latin can still be enjoyed by students, even though they cannot go to a country to practice the language.

Why study Latin at all, you might ask? Is there a good reason to spend time learning its vocabulary and expressions? You may be surprised to learn how helpful Latin can be. As you study the language, you will recognize the Latin roots of many English words. The more Latin you learn, the more you will see the close relationship between many Latin and English words. The more Latin you know, the better your understanding and mastery of English vocabulary. Latin is even more closely related to other Romance languages you will study in this course or later.

You may have noticed the similarity between the word *Romance* and the word *Roman*. Spanish, French, and Italian are called Romance languages because they stem from the language spoken by the Romans — Latin.

Latin also appears in the language of the courts. All good lawyers must know Latin phrases to help their clients. Likewise, doctors learn Latin as they study medical terminology. Latin can also help you with your study of history because much of the history important to the Western world began in the Latin-speaking world of the Romans. Someday you may even learn enough Latin to be able to read fine Roman literature in its original language.

Learning Latin gives you a sense of the beginnings of your culture, your cultural roots. For centuries, knowing Latin has been one of the hallmarks of an educated person. If you know Latin, you are in very good company.

1. What was the name of the empire where Latin was spoken? _____

2. Which three continents included parts of the Roman Empire? _____

   _____

3. Which country had the greatest influence on Roman civilization? _____

4. Who were Julius Caesar and Augustus? _____

   _____

5. What was the **Pax Romana**? _____

   _____

6. Which emperor "fiddled while Rome burnt?" _____

7. Name the first Christian emperor of Rome. _____

8. What tribe conquered Rome? _____

9. How did the Romance languages receive their name?

   _____

   _____

10. Name at least two ways in which the study of Latin can be helpful to you now. _____

    _____

    _____

II Latin Cognates

You already know many Latin words. Some of the words are spelled exactly like English: **album, animal, actor, color**. Many other words are spelled almost the same in English and Latin. Here are some clues to watch for. Many Latin words ending in **-a** frequently end in *-e* or drop **-a** in English: **musica** = *music*, **Europa** = *Europe*. Latin words ending in **-ia** often end in *-y* in English: **familia** = *family*, **Germania** = *Germany*. Words ending in **-us** in Latin sometimes end in *-e* or drop **-us** in English: **insanus** = *insane*, **Augustus** = *August*.

How many of the following Latin words can you recognize? Fill in the blanks with the English meanings. If you need to, you may look in a dictionary. Listen to your teacher for the pronunciation of these words:

1. activitas_____
2. adultus _____
3. album_____
4. Aprilis _____
5. athleta _____
6. camelus_____
7. candela _____
8. causa _____
9. defendere _____
10. difficilis_____

11. enormis _____
12. famosus _____
13. Februarius_____
14. forma _____
15. fortuna _____
16. gloria _____
17. honestus _____
18. hora _____
19. immortalis_____
20. incredibilis _____

21. Italia _____

22. libertas _____

23. medicina _____

24. memoria _____

25. monstrum _____

26. natura _____

27. necessarius _____

28. occasio _____

29. oceanus _____

30. odor _____

31. oliva _____

32. opinio _____

33. ornamentum _____

34. parentes _____

35. patientia _____

36. persona _____

37. philosophia _____

38. planeta _____

39. religio _____

40. Romanus _____

41. rosa _____

42. ruina _____

43. sandalium _____

44. schola _____

45. stomachus _____

46. stupidus _____

47. symphonia _____

48. terribilis _____

49. theatrum _____

50. tigris _____

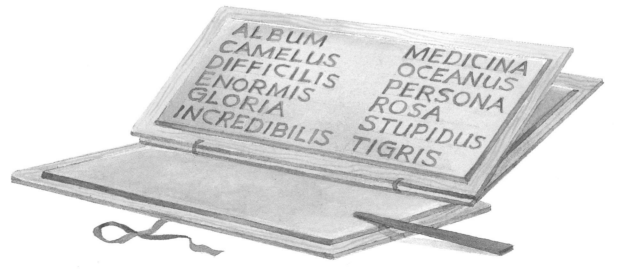

Romans as Builders

The Romans were great builders of roads and waterways. They paved the roads of their cities and built a network of roads to connect the important centers of the Empire. These roads allowed for quick transportation of troops as well as cheap and easy transportation of goods. The ability to travel and easily move within the Roman territories enabled the Romans to maintain control over their large empire. The solid construction and durable materials used to build these roads have preserved some of them to this day.

The Romans also created ingenious methods of bringing water to the cities. Aqueducts were built to transport water over miles of land. The water ran in open channels across the top of the aqueducts. Some were over thirty miles long and three stories high. Water from the aqueducts was channeled through pipes to various parts of the town. The aqueducts enabled the Romans to provide water for more people, making it possible for cities to expand and grow.

The Romans used water not only for drinking but also for purposes that modern western civilization adopted much later. A few homes had running water for baths and toilets. Public lavatories and bath houses used running water for sanitary and more pleasant facilities.

III Latin Names

Now that you are able to recognize over 50 Latin words resembling English, let's look at how Latin and English names compare.

Claudia is going to help you learn how to pronounce some of these names.

You will meet **Claudia** throughout this book holding up her writing tablet with one or two pronunciation clues she wants to share with you as you develop a good Latin pronunciation.

Whenever you look at **Claudia**'s clues, keep this in mind: every time you try to pronounce a Latin sound, hold your mouth, tongue, lips, and teeth in the same position at the end of the sound as you did at the beginning. Try saying **o** this way. Now try **oooo**. There, you've got it.

Claudia has two clues for you before you look at the following list of boys' and girls' names. These clues tell you how to pronounce HER name:

causa, **Aurora**   campus, Cornelia

Here is a list of boys' and girls' names. With your teacher's help, choose a Latin name that you would like to have for yourself while you are studying Latin:

Antonius	Horatius	Marcellus	Messala
Aurelius	Livius	Marcus	Octavius
Balbus	Lucius	Maximus	Paquius
Caius			Paullus
Cicero			Petronius
Claudius			Plinius
Clemens			Quintus
Crassus			Rufus
Davus			Seneca
Domitius			Sextus
Drusus			Tiberius
Faustus			Titus
Furius			Tullius
Gaius			Valerius
Gallus			Virgilius

Agrippina	Julia	Lucia	Maria
Antonia	Junia	Lucretia	Marica
Appia	Livia	Marcia	Maxima
Aurelia			Octavia
Aurora			Pompeia
Caecilia			Porcia
Cassia			Quintilia
Claudia			Sabina
Diana			Sempronia
Domitia			Silvia
Drusilla			Sulpicia
Fausta			Tiberia
Flavia			Tullia
Fulvia			Valeria
Gaia			Virginia

ACTIVITAS

When the Romans wanted to say, "My name is Antonia," they would say, **"Mihi nomen est Antonia."** Practice telling your teacher and your classmates your name in Latin. If you and your teacher have chosen Latin names, use them.

Mihi nomen est Antonia.

Claudia's clues:

a = a in father
e = e in bed
i = ee in see

Mihi nomen est Antonia.

Dialogus I   *Salve*

* Masculine names ending in **-us**, like **Marcus**, change **-us** to **-e** when speaking to the person.

ACTIVITAS

1. Salve, _____ (name).

   Salve, _____ (name).

2. Quod nomen est tibi?

   Mihi nomen est _____. Et tibi?

3. Quid agis?
   Valeo, gratias. Quid agis tu?

4. Ego quoque valeo. Vale.

   Vale.

Toys and Games

Roman children, much like boys and girls of your age, enjoyed playing games and had fun with a variety of toys. Children played leapfrog, jumped rope, spun tops, played jacks, rode on swings, played catch, played with dolls, and rolled hoops. Board games similar to chess and checkers were also very popular as were other board games played with dice. Boys played various games of ball, including a game like field hockey.

Children also liked to play make-believe games like playing school or playing soldier and gladiator with toy wooden swords. They also had great fun imitating a favorite adult game: chariot racing. They would use a cart or little chariot big enough for a child and have it pulled by a dog, a goat, or a donkey.

Girls played with dolls made of cloth. Dolls were also made of wood or bone and sometimes had arms and legs that could move. Girls, on the night before their wedding, dedicated their toys to the family gods who had protected them during childhood.

IV Numbers

Claudia's clues:

o = o in hope

u = u in rude

du**o**, n**o**vem

du**o**, quatt**u**or

You will soon be able to count to forty in Latin. Listen to your teacher to learn how to pronounce the numbers 1 to 20.

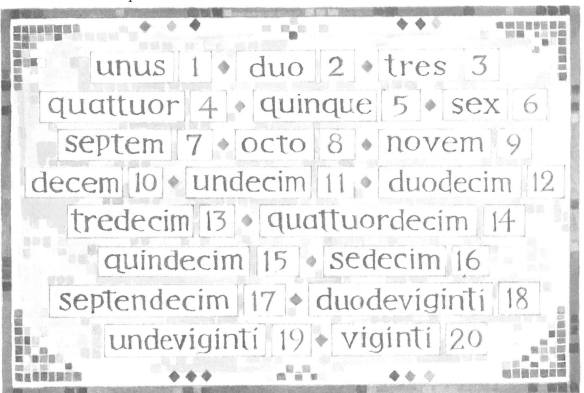

unus 1 ◆ duo 2 ◆ tres 3
quattuor 4 ◆ quinque 5 ◆ sex 6
septem 7 ◆ octo 8 ◆ novem 9
decem 10 ◆ undecim 11 ◆ duodecim 12
tredecim 13 ◆ quattuordecim 14
quindecim 15 ◆ sedecim 16
septendecim 17 ◆ duodeviginti 18
undeviginti 19 ◆ viginti 20

1. Cover the Latin number words and say the numbers aloud in Latin.

2. Now cover the Latin number words and write the Latin number words in the blank lines.

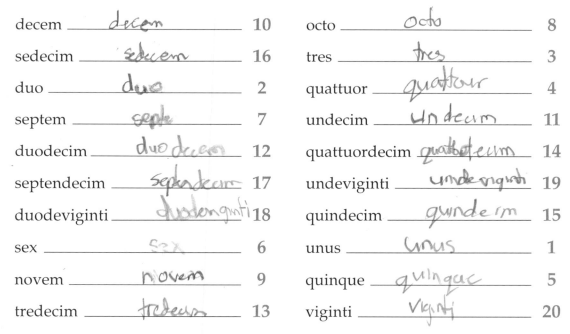

decem	_decem_	10
sedecim	_sedecem_	16
duo	_duo_	2
septem	_sepe_	7
duodecim	_duo decem_	12
septendecim	_sepedecim_	17
duodeviginti	_duodenginti_	18
sex	_sex_	6
novem	_novem_	9
tredecim	_tredecm_	13

octo	_octo_	8
tres	_tres_	3
quattuor	_quattour_	4
undecim	_Undecim_	11
quattuordecim	_quatbdecim_	14
undeviginti	_undevginti_	19
quindecim	_gwindecim_	15
unus	_Unus_	1
quinque	_quinquic_	5
viginti	_viginti_	20

3. Pretend you are the teacher and correct your work with a red pen or pencil. You will be able to see at a glance which words you need to study further.

ACTIVITAS

Your teacher will read some Latin numbers from 1 to 20 in random order to you. Write the numerals for the number you hear:

1. _____   4. _____   7. _____   10. _____

2. _____   5. _____   8. _____   11. _____

3. _____   6. _____   9. _____   12. _____

Let's continue learning numbers. Listen to your teacher to learn how to say the numbers 21 to 40.

viginti unus 21
viginti duo 22 • viginti tres 23
viginti quattuor 24
viginti quinque 25 • viginti sex 26
viginti septem 27
duodetriginta 28
undetriginta 29
triginta 30
triginta unus 31
triginta duo 32
triginta tres 33
triginta quattuor 34
triginta quinque 35
triginta sex 36
triginta septem 37
duodequadraginta 38
undequadraginta 39
quadraginta 40

Your teacher will read some numbers from 21 to 40 in random order to you. Write the numerals for the Latin number you hear:

1. _____   6. _____

2. _____   7. _____

3. _____   8. _____

4. _____   9. _____

5. _____   10. _____

Now see how many Latin number words you can recognize. Draw a line to match the Latin number word with its numeral:

undequadraginta	40
undetriginta	34
duodetriginta	21
quadraginta	36
triginta quattuor	23
triginta duo	28
triginta sex	32
viginti unus	39
viginti sex	26
viginti tres	29

Roman Numerals

Here are the basic Roman numerals with their equivalent Arabic numerals:

I = 1	**X** = 10	**C** = 100	**M** = 1000
V = 5	**L** = 50	**D** = 500	

As you can see, the Romans used letters of the alphabet to represent numbers. Different combinations of Roman numerals can form any number. You need only a few simple rules:

1. To make a numeral larger, place one, two, or three smaller numerals after it:

VI = 6	**VII** = 7	**VIII** = 8
XI = 11	**XII** = 12	**XIII** = 13
CX = 110	**DL** = 550	**MC** = 1100

2. To make a numeral smaller, place a smaller numeral in front of it:

IV = 4	**IX** = 9	**XC** = 90	**CM** = 900

3. Repeat a numeral to double or triple its value:

XX = 20	**XXX** = 30
CC = 200	**CCC** = 300
MM = 2,000	

Roman numerals from **I** (1) to **MM** (2,000)

I	1	**VI**	6	**XI**	11	**XVI**	16
II	2	**VII**	7	**XII**	12	**XVII**	17
III	3	**VIII**	8	**XIII**	13	**XVIII**	18
IV	4	**IX**	9	**XIV**	14	**XIX**	19
V	5	**X**	10	**XV**	15	**XX**	20

XXI	21	**L**	50	**LXXI**	71	**C**	100
XXX	30	**LI**	51	**LXXX**	80	**CI**	101
XXXI	31	**LX**	60	**LXXXI**	81	**CC**	200
XL	40	**LXI**	61	**XC**	90	**CCI**	201
XLI	41	**LXX**	70	**XCI**	91	**CCC**	300

CCCI	301	**DI**	501	**DCCI**	701	**CMI**	901
CD	400	**DC**	600	**DCCC**	800	**M**	1,000
CDI	401	**DCI**	601	**DCCCI**	801	**MI**	1,001
D	500	**DCC**	700	**CM**	900	**MM**	2,000

Give the corresponding Arabic numeral for the following:

Example: XI = __12__

1. CCC = _____   **4.** XXV = _____   **7.** CC = _____

2. IX = _____   **5.** CD = _____   **8.** CMII = _____

3. MC = _____   **6.** LXXIV = _____

Give the corresponding Roman numeral for the following:

Example: 12 = __XII__

1. 59 = _____   **3.** 42 = _____   **5.** 290 = _____

2. 85 = _____   **4.** 101 = _____   **6.** 1610 = _____

Roman arithmetic. Write the problem and give the answer in Roman numerals:

Example: 3 + 1 = __III + I = IV__

1. 4 + 5 = _____   **4.** 10 – 4 = _____

2. 10 + 20 = _____   **5.** 500 – 400 = _____

3. 50 + 80 = _____   **6.** 1000 – 100 = _____

Now that you know the numbers from 1 to 40, write the Latin number words for the Roman numerals. Then find the correct answers in the puzzle. Circle them from left to right, right to left, up or down, or diagonally:

1. XXXVI _____

2. XL _____

3. IV _____

4. XXII _____

5. I _____

6. XXXIX _____

7. XX _____

8. X _____

9. XIX _____

10. XI _____

11. XVI _____

12. XXIX _____

13. VII _____

14. XXX _____

15. V _____

16. XVII _____

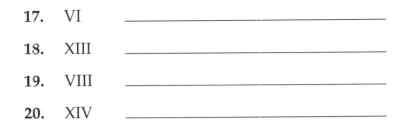

17. VI   _____

18. XIII   _____

19. VIII   _____

20. XIV   _____

```
U N D E Q U A D R A G I N T A
Q U M O V I T N I G I V T R P
A T N I G I R T E D N U R U U
X A R E C C A R T H V R E O A
E G U N D E C I M D E U D U T
S E P T E N D E C I M N E M N
A S E N D A E R S T P U C E I
T I A S A U C I O V I S I P G
N D S E P T E M R U I S M D A
I A V D O U Q U A T T U O R R
G E X E O T R I G I N T A E D
I D E C E M I X E T I N A X A
R O T I T N I G I V E D N U U
T O A M V I G I N T I D U O Q
M U Q U I N Q U E R S E X E T
```

VI Days of the Week

Claudia's clues:

ae = y in my

j = y in yes

lun**ae**, Caecilia

Junia, Julia

dies Solis	dies Lunae	dies Martis	dies Mercurii	dies Jovis	dies Veneris	dies Saturni
I	II	III	IV	V	VI	VII
VIII	IX	X	XI	XII	XIII	XIV
XV	XVI	XVII	XVIII	XIX	XX	XXI
XXII	XXIII	XXIV	XXV	XXVI	XXVII	XXVIII
XXIX	XXX	XXXI				

These are the days of the week in Latin. The first word means *day of* and is not capitalized; the second word is the name of a god or celestial body and is capitalized.

Hodie est dies Lunae. = *Today is Monday.*

Each day, find as many people as you can and tell them the day of the week in Latin.

Cover page 24 with a sheet of paper. Can you fill in the days that come before and after the days given?

1. _____

   dies Veneris

   _____

2. _____

   dies Lunae

   _____

3. _____

   dies Mercurii

   _____

4. _____

   dies Solis

   _____

Capsula culturae

Food

What did the Romans eat? The Romans had a varied diet of eggs, meat, vegetables, and fruits. Bread was essential to a meal. Milk and cheese were common foods, as were beans, cabbage, and onions. Fruits — mostly grapes, apples, figs, and pears — were eaten fresh, and figs and grapes were also dried for the winter. Pork was the favorite meat, although fresh and salted fish, poultry, and game meat, like birds and even peacocks, were also popular. Oysters were a favorite delicacy of the wealthy. Olive oil was used in cooking, in oil lamps for lighting, and rubbed on the skin for cleansing. Honey was used for sweetening. Wine was a popular drink. It was usually drunk mixed with water or honey at all meals. Dessert included fruit, nuts, and sweets.

The main meal of the day was dinner. It generally started around 3 or 4 o'clock and sometimes lasted several hours. The wealthy enjoyed a three-course meal, while the poor ate beans, vegetables, cheese, and bread and drank cheap wine.

Romans served food on plates and in bowls made of bronze, silver, or earthenware. They drank from cups, bowls, or chalices. Forks were rarely used; instead, Romans used spoons and, more commonly, their fingers. Meat was cut before being served. Finger bowls and napkins were available at the table to wash the hands.

Romans did not sit at a table for meals, and chairs were uncommon in the Roman home. The preferred sitting place was the couch, which was used not only for reading and relaxation but also for eating. Long couches around the table allowed both men and women to stretch out comfortably and to enjoy their meal and company leisurely.

VII Months of the Year

The months of the year in Latin resemble English. Can you recognize all of them?

JANUARIUS · FEBRUARIUS · MARTIUS

APRILIS · MAIUS · JUNIUS

JULIUS · AUGUSTUS · SEPTEMBER

OCTOBER · NOVEMBER · DECEMBER

Unscramble the letters to form the name of a Latin month:

1. VOBERMEN

2. SIJULU

3. REFUSIABUR

4. RIPILAS

5. SUITMRA

6. COREBOT

7. SUARJUANI

8. MECDEBER

9. SUMIA

10. REPEBSTEM

11. GUASTUSU

12. SUNJUI

Match the names of the months with their numbers by drawing lines between the two columns. For example, January is number one and December is number twelve:

Aprilis	undecim
Augustus	unus
December	decem
Februarius	duo
Julius	duodecim
Junius	novem
Januarius	octo
Maius	quinque
Martius	quattuor
November	septem
October	sex
September	tres

Fill in the blanks with the correct Latin names of the days or months, then find the nineteen names of the day or month in the puzzle. Circle them from left to right, right to left, up or down, or diagonally:

1. The month of Memorial Day: _____

2. The second day of your
   school week: *dies* _____

3. The month of Thanksgiving: _____

4. Many people go to church
   on this day of the week: *dies* _____

5. The first day of the weekend: *dies* _____

6. The month when winter begins: _____

7. The first day of the school week: *dies* _____

8. Halloween is on the last
   day of this month: _____

9. The day after Tuesday: *dies* _____

10. The month of the
    United States' birthday: _____

11. The last day of your school week: *dies* _____

12. The month of the autumnal
    equinox when fall begins: _____

13. The month of St. Patrick's Day: _____

14. The day after Wednesday: *dies* _____

15. The last month of your school year: _____

16. The first month of the year: _____

17. The month of April Fool's Day: _____

18. The month of Valentine's Day: _____

19. The month after July: _____

Claudia's clue:

$g = g$ in go

agis, ago

Dialogus II *Quid est?*

* Latin, unlike English, has neither definite nor indefinite articles. There are no Latin words for *the*, *a*, or *an*.

Now let's review what you learned in Dialog II:

1. Salve, _____ (name of friend). Quid

agis?

2. Valeo, tibi ago gratias. Quid novi?

Nihil novi.

3. Quid est?

_____ est.

4. Multas gratias.

Capsula culturae

Life and Work

In early Roman history, the main occupation was farming. With the introduction of slave labor, larger farms replaced smaller farms. As landless Romans flocked to the city in search of a living, cities grew in population and size. At the height of its greatness, over one million people lived in Rome. In the cities, men learned one of the many crafts and trades available. Weavers, shoemakers, blacksmiths, gold and silversmiths, potters, bakers, barbers, stonemasons, and carpenters were in great demand.

Craftsmen led a hard life. They worked long hours and received low wages, unless they were very skilled in their craft. With their families, they lived in crowded, dingy apartments consisting of a room or two in badly constructed buildings as high as four or five stories. These buildings could be easily destroyed by fire or simply collapsed because of faulty construction. If you walked the narrow, winding streets of ancient Rome, you would see small workshops, stores, and eating places on the ground floor of most houses.

The hard life of the common craftsman and tradesman was much different from the comfortable life of the upper classes. They became rich with trade, real estate, and tax collecting. The households of the rich were run by dozens of servants, each specializing in a household duty, from polishing silver to weaving wool for the family. The wealthy Roman family lived in large, comfortable town houses decorated with rugs and draperies. The walls were covered with elaborate paintings. The gardens, surrounded by columns, included fountains and statues. The wealthy also had country houses, where they vacationed in summer.

VIII The Classroom

Claudia's clues:

charta, stomachus

cathedra

Can you imagine a typical classroom of two thousand years ago? Lessons were not held in a classroom but on an open porch. Students did not sit at desks but on a **subsellium** (*bench*) and held their materials on their laps. Roman students "wrote" on their wax **tabula** (*tablet*) that consisted of wooden boards covered with a thin layer of wax. They wrote by scratching the wax with a pointed stylus made of wood, bone, or steel. The other end of the stylus was flat for smoothing over the wax or "erasing." The **tabula** could be erased easily and used many times over.

Occasionally, students wrote on a sheet of expensive **charta** (*paper*) made from papyrus leaves, a water plant found mainly in Egypt. They wrote with a **calamus** (*pen*) dipped in **atramentum** (*ink*). Roman students did not study from books but from a **volumen** (*scroll*), which consisted of a continuous roll of papyrus.

Learn the names of the objects of a Roman classroom. See how many names you can remember at a time without having to look at the book.

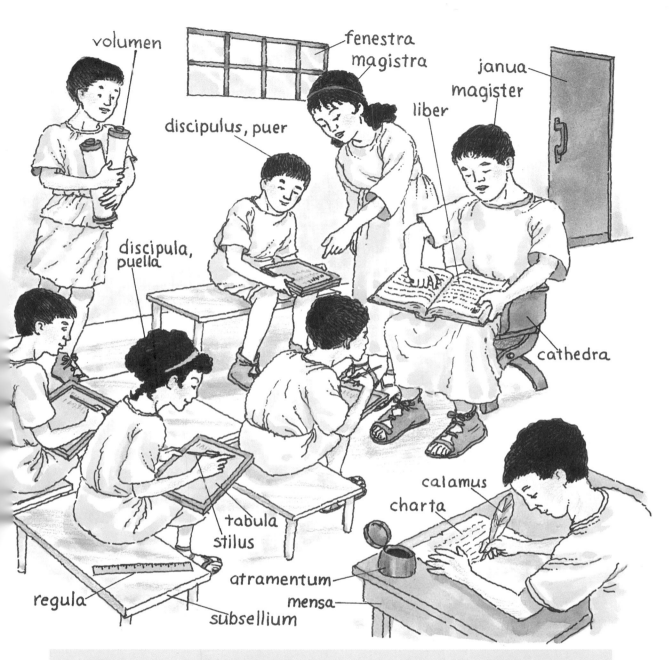

volumen

fenestra
magistra

janua
magister

discipulus, puer

liber

discipula,
puella

cathedra

calamus
charta

tabula
stilus

atramentum

regula

mensa

subsellium

In Latin, every noun, or name of object, is considered masculine, feminine, or neuter. (The Latin word **neuter** means *neither*.) How do you tell the gender of nouns? The endings of Latin words often give a clue to their gender. For example, nouns ending in **-a**, like **janua** and **tabula**, are usually feminine; nouns ending in **-us**, like **calamus**, are usually masculine; and nouns ending in **-um**, like **subsellium**, are usually neuter.

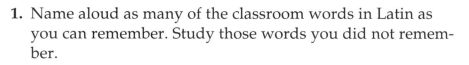

1. Name aloud as many of the classroom words in Latin as you can remember. Study those words you did not remember.

2. Write the names of the illustrations in Latin in the first column of blank lines.

3. Correct your work. Give yourself one point for each correct answer.

4. Now cover the illustrations and write the English meanings of the Latin words in the second column of blank lines.

5. Correct your work. Give yourself one point for each correct answer.

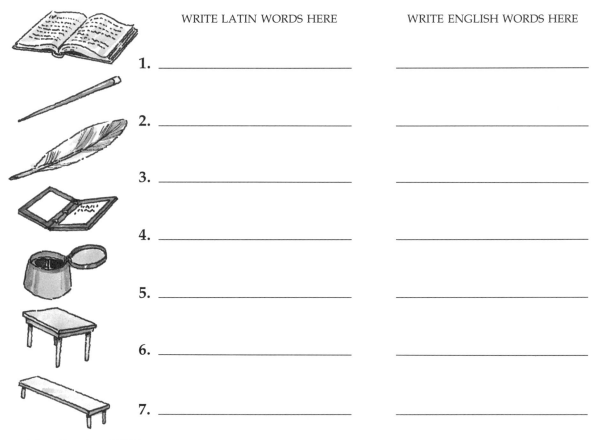

WRITE LATIN WORDS HERE   WRITE ENGLISH WORDS HERE

1. _____   _____

2. _____   _____

3. _____   _____

4. _____   _____

5. _____   _____

6. _____   _____

7. _____   _____

WRITE LATIN WORDS HERE   WRITE ENGLISH WORDS HERE

8. _____   _____

9. _____   _____

10. _____   _____

11. _____   _____

12. _____   _____

13. _____   _____

14. _____   _____

15. _____   _____

16. _____   _____

17. _____   _____

Thirty-four points is a perfect score. If you made a mistake, you can improve your score by repeating the exercise on a blank piece of paper and correcting it again.

Classroom Vocabulary Puzzle: To solve this puzzle, first express the following words in Latin, then fit them in the puzzle vertically and horizontally:

5-letter words

book ___ ___ ___ ___ ___

door ___ ___ ___ ___ ___

table ___ ___ ___ ___ ___

6-letter words

girl ___ ___ ___ ___ ___ ___

paper ___ ___ ___ ___ ___ ___

ruler ___ ___ ___ ___ ___ ___

stylus ___ ___ ___ ___ ___ ___

writing tablet ___ ___ ___ ___ ___ ___

7-letter words

pen ___ ___ ___ ___ ___ ___ ___

scroll ___ ___ ___ ___ ___ ___ ___

8-letter words

female teacher ___ ___ ___ ___ ___ ___ ___ ___

male teacher ___ ___ ___ ___ ___ ___ ___ ___

teacher's chair ___ ___ ___ ___ ___ ___ ___ ___

window ___ ___ ___ ___ ___ ___ ___ ___

10-letter words

bench ___ ___ ___ ___ ___ ___ ___ ___ ___ ___

ink ___ ___ ___ ___ ___ ___ ___ ___ ___ ___

male student ___ ___ ___ ___ ___ ___ ___ ___ ___ ___

Capsula culturae

Roman Education

In early Roman times, children received their education at home from tutors and parents. Mothers taught girls how to manage the home, and fathers taught boys to fight in armor, box, ride a horse, hunt, and play sports.

Later, schoolmasters set up schools in their homes. Boys and girls whose families could afford it attended school beginning at the age of 6 or 7. Although girls were allowed to attend school, few did. Most girls continued to be educated at home since they did not require skills to pursue careers outside the home.

Young Roman students studied the three R's: reading, writing, and 'rithmetic. They were often taught to the tune of a hickory stick. Strict schoolteachers did not hesitate to whip them if they misbehaved or did not study.

Older students studied Greek and Roman literature, philosophy, history, geography, advanced mathematics, law and public speaking, music, and astronomy.

Roman parents, especially in wealthy families, placed great importance on education. They encouraged their sons, from as early as three years of age, to learn to read, write, and do math. Although some young men continued their education past grade school, most Roman boys completed only elementary school and then learned a trade.

When you want to talk about yourself in Latin, you will need to know the names of the parts of the body. How many names can you remember without having to look at the book?

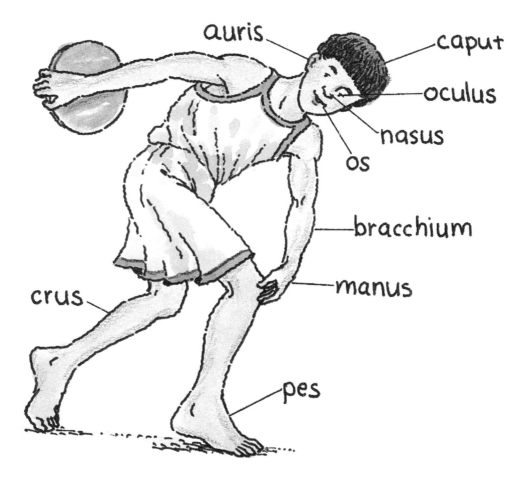

auris

caput

oculus

nasus

os

bracchium

manus

crus

pes

Fill in the names of the parts of the body:

Choose a partner. Point to each other's hand, foot, and so on, and ask, **"Quid est?"** Answer, **"Manus est." "Pes est."** And so on.

Complete this crossword puzzle with the Latin names of the parts of the body:

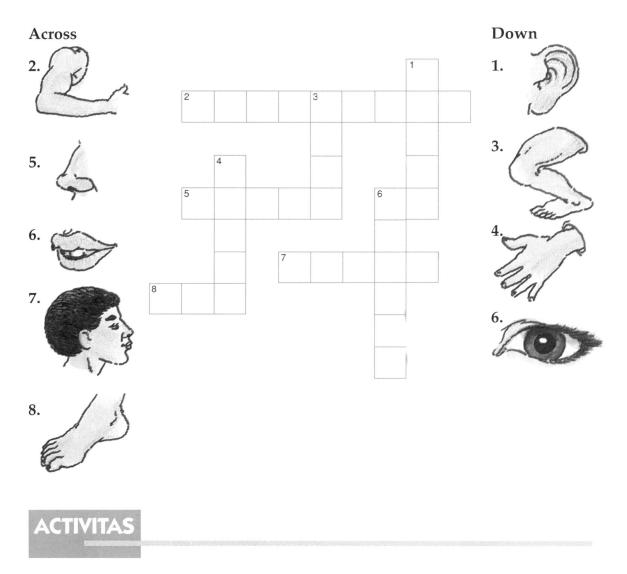

Across

2.

5.

6.

7.

8.

Down

1.

3.

4.

6.

"Simon dicit" means "Simon says." Move or point to that part of the body Simon refers to only if you hear the words **"Simon dicit."** If you do not hear the words **"Simon dicit,"** don't move at all.

Capsula culturae

Roman Fashions

Roman clothing was very simple. The basic article of clothing for both men and women was the tunic (**tunica**), a long, loose-fitting shirt with short sleeves. It was usually made of white wool and worn with a belt around the waist. Everyone wore a white tunic, including boys and girls. The tunics of senators and generals were distinguished by purple stripes down the front and back. Wool was the most common fabric, followed by linen. Silk was rare and expensive, and cotton was almost unknown. In cold weather, it was common to wear several tunics on top of one another or a heavy woolen cloak.

On formal occasions, Roman citizens wore a **toga**. Important citizens always wore togas in public, and only Roman citizens were allowed to wear them at all. Judges and boys under sixteen years of age wore togas with a purple trim around its edges. The toga, a large semi-circular piece of white fabric, was draped over the left shoulder, under the right arm, and again over the left shoulder. Large as a blanket, the toga was cumbersome and not the easiest piece of clothing to wear, but citizens wore it with pride because it distinguished them as Roman citizens.

Married women wore a long dress gathered just above the waist called a **stola**. The **stola** was worn over the tunic. Sometimes a decorative shawl or a cloak was added for warmth. Stolas were dyed in a variety of colors — purple, red, blue, green, and yellow. Generally, women's clothing was also made of wool or linen, but wealthy Roman women occasionally used imported silks from China or cotton from India.

Sandals and slippers were worn indoors and shoes outdoors. Officials wore red shoes. No socks or stockings were worn, but in winter feet were sometimes wrapped in strips of cloth.

After scissors and sharp razors were introduced, Roman men cut their hair and shaved regularly. Young men did not shave their first fuzz but allowed it to grow to almost a beard. A young man's first shave was celebrated as a solemn family affair.

Roman women spent much time and money on beauty. Women wore their hair long in constantly changing and very elaborate styles. Colored ribbons and beautifully ornate pins on the hair were a common practice. False hair, wigs, and dyes were also widely used by women and frequently by men as well. Roman women also wore make-up, including lipstick, eye shadow, and mascara. They plucked their eyebrows and manicured their nails. Women also wore false teeth. To keep their skin soft, they used face creams and perfumed olive oil. Soaps were unknown to the Romans, but scents and oils were extremely popular with both men and women.

Women also enjoyed wearing jewelry. Bracelets, worn on the upper arm, necklaces, pins, and earrings were made of gold, silver, and bronze. Rings were favored by both women and men.

Talking About Yourself

An adjective describes a person or thing. In the sentence "The tall girl is strong," *tall* and *strong* are adjectives that describe *girl*. Many adjectives are easy to remember if you think of them in pairs:

intellegens   stupidus   maestus   laetus

parvus   procerus   pulcher   turpis

validus   infirmus   crassus   tenuis

amicus   malignus

Cover page 48 with a sheet of paper. Write the Latin adjectives that describe the people and animals you see:

1. _____

2. _____

3. _____

4. _____

5. _____

6. _____

7. _____

8. _____

9. _____

10. _____

11. _____

12. _____

13. _____

14. _____

Dialogus III *Ego sum . . .*

Let's take a closer look at some of the words you learned in Dialog III:

Ego sum . . .

Tu es . . .

Is est . . .

Puer est . . .

Ea est . . .

Puella est . . .

Look at the adjectives on the left that could describe a boy. Compare them with the adjectives on the right that could describe a girl:

amicus	amica
crassus	crassa
infirmus	infirma
laetus	laeta
maestus	maesta
malignus	maligna
parvus	parva
procerus	procera
stupidus	stupida
validus	valida

Latin adjectives, like Latin nouns, have a gender. A feminine adjective is used to describe a feminine noun and a masculine adjective is used to describe a masculine noun. How do we change a masculine adjective to get the feminine?

Use as many adjectives on page 53 as possible to describe these animals:

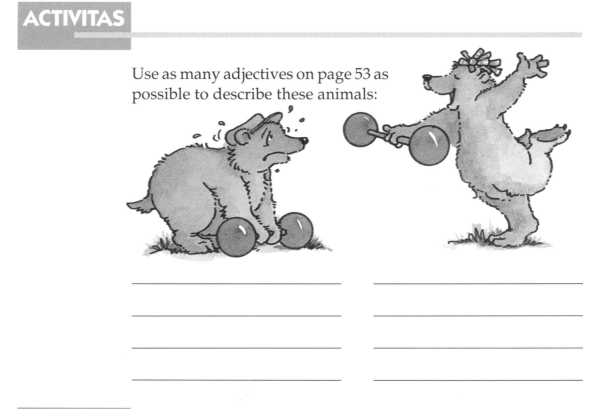

_____   _____

_____   _____

_____   _____

_____   _____

ACTIVITAS

You have already learned that changing the **-us** ending of a Latin adjective to **-a** gives you the feminine form. Now let's learn about the feminine forms of other adjectives. Adjectives ending in **-is** — like **tenuis** and **turpis** — and the adjective **intellegens** do not change in the feminine.

Let's practice these adjectives by filling in the blanks with the adjective that describes the people and animals in the pictures:

1. Tigris est _____ .

Rufa est _____ .

2. Is est _____ .

Ea quoque est _____ .

3. Marcus est _____ .

Silvia quoque est _____ .

Finally let's look at adjectives ending in **-er**, like **pulcher**. The **-er** of **pulcher** changes to **-ra** to form the feminine. Now fill in the blanks and describe the boy and girl in this illustration:

4. Is est puer _____ .

Ea est puella _____ .

1. How many of the boys in this ball team can you describe? Write the adjective that best describes each player next to his number in the column of blank lines:

PUERI

I	_____
II	_____
III	_____
IV	_____
V	_____
VI	_____
VII	_____
VIII	_____
IX	_____
X	_____
XI	_____
XII	_____

2. How would you change the adjectives to describe each player of the opposing girls' team? Write the adjective that best describes each player next to her number in the column of blank lines:

PUELLAE

I	_____
II	_____
III	_____
IV	_____
V	_____
VI	_____
VII	_____
VIII	_____
IX	_____
X	_____
XI	_____
XII	_____

ACTIVITAS

Your teacher will now divide you into small groups to practice describing yourself and one another.

ACTIVITAS

Play charades with the adjectives you have learned. Your teacher will divide the class into teams, and a member from one team will stand in front of the class and act out the various ways he or she would look if sad, intelligent, fat, and so on.

Capsula culturae

Sports

The Romans were a fun-loving people. Much of their leisure time was spent watching sporting events, gladiatorial shows, circus acts, and theater. Romans also enjoyed listening to music often played by traveling musicians in the streets or by professionals in concerts held in wealthy homes.

Although organized sport teams representing cities or schools did not exist, it was very common for wealthy citizens and public officials to sponsor games and amusements. They celebrated religious festivals, military victories, election campaigns, and even funerals. Games and shows included boxing and wrestling matches and circus acts — acrobats, jugglers, tight-rope walkers. Admission to all events was free, and anyone could attend.

Among the favorite shows were the gladiator fights. Gladiators fought on the ground or on horseback with daggers and shields, their bodies covered with armor. Some gladiators even fought blindfolded for the amusement of the spectators. Fights between gladiators and wild animals — lions, bears, elephants, and rhinos — were also popular.

The popularity of these spectacles encouraged the building of large amphitheaters and stadiums able to seat thousands of spectators. The largest and greatest stadium ever built is the Colosseum in Rome, which exists to this day. It was an architectural marvel for its time and could hold 50,000 spectators.

Also very popular were the chariot races. Men riding chariots pulled by as many as four horses drove around a track. Chariot drivers were popular heroes and often became rich. The biggest stadium for holding chariot races was the Circus Maximus in Rome, which could hold 250,000 spectators, more than any football stadium in the world.

Theater was another form of entertainment loved by the Romans, who based much of their drama on Greek plays. Actors wore masks for the characters they played, and women's roles were played by men. Audiences particularly liked comedies and farces in which actors played ridiculous and funny situations. Romans also told stories with mime, a form of silent drama they invented. These stories were performed on wooden stages set up in the street. They were a favorite of the common people.

XI Animals and Colors

Can you recognize all these animals? Listen to your teacher to learn how to say the Latin names of animals. How many animals can you remember without looking at the book?

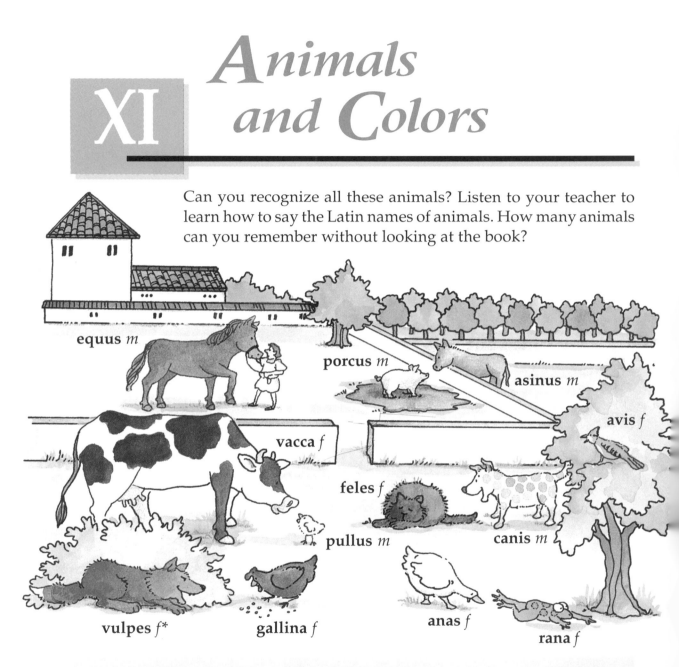

equus *m*

porcus *m*

asinus *m*

avis *f*

vacca *f*

feles *f*

pullus *m*

canis *m*

vulpes *f**

gallina *f*

anas *f*

rana *f*

* You have already learned that Latin nouns have gender and that nouns ending in **-a**, like **gallina**, are usually feminine and nouns ending in **-us**, like **pullus**, are usually masculine. We say *usually* because certain nouns do not fall into these groups. From now on, the gender will be indicated with the letter *f* for feminine nouns and *m* for masculine nouns.

Which of these animals do you like best? List animals in Latin according to your preferences. Start with your favorite animal and end with your least favorite:

anas	canis	gallina	rana
asinus	equus	porcus	vacca
avis	feles	pullus	vulpes

1. _____

2. _____

3. _____

4. _____

5. _____

6. _____

7. _____

8. _____

9. _____

10. _____

11. _____

12. _____

Can you describe the animals in the pictures on the next page? Remember to use feminine adjectives with feminine nouns. Here are two examples to get you started:

Gallina est maesta.

Pullus est laetus.

1. _____ 2. _____

3. _____ 4. _____

5. _____ 6. _____

7. _____ 8. _____

9. _____ 10. _____

Now let's learn some Latin color words. What is the color of these animals? Listen to your teacher read the description under each animal. Find the animals and guess the meaning of the Latin color words. Here is an example to get you started:

Porcus est rosaceus. = *The pig is pink.*

Asinus est canus.

Equus est fuscus.

Porcus est rosaceus.

Avis est caerulea.

Vacca est alba et atra.

Pullus est flavus.

Feles est atra.

Vulpes est rubra.

Anas est alba.

Rana est prasina.

Since color words are adjectives, they agree in gender with the animal they describe. What gender are the color words **rubra**, **prasina**, **alba**, and **atra**? Can you guess the masculine forms of these adjectives? Write the masculine forms in the blanks:

FEMININE	MASCULINE		FEMININE	MASCULINE
rubra	_____		prasina	_____
alba	_____		atra	_____

ACTIVITAS

Let's practice the color words you learned. Color each bowl of paint on this artist's table according to the color indicated:

ACTIVITAS

Find the hidden animals. There are 12 animals hidden in the picture on the next page. Find the animals and color them a color you can say in Latin. Colors can be repeated.

Then look at the picture you colored and write twelve sentences to indicate the color of the animals.

Examples: **Canus est ruber.**
              Vacca est flava.

Since you have to know the name of the animal *and* the color, give yourself two points for each animal you described correctly. You can earn a total of twenty-four points. Perhaps your teacher would like you and a classmate to correct each other's work.

1. _____   7. _____

2. _____   8. _____

3. _____   9. _____

4. _____   10. _____

5. _____   11. _____

6. _____   12. _____

Capsula culturae

Roman Baths

Most people in Rome lived in apartments, which had no toilets or bathrooms. Only the homes of the rich contained a toilet with running water, a remarkable feat for the times.

Public baths were one of the most important centers of Roman life. All Romans used them, not only for cleanliness and health but also for relaxation and fun. Initially simple and often dingy structures, the baths gradually became more elaborate and pleasant. In addition to bathing facilities with running hot and cold water, saunas, and massage rooms, some of the more lavish baths also had lounges for chatting, libraries, reading rooms, snack shops, barbershops, and exercise rooms.

The largest bath of the Roman Empire could hold 30,000 bathers and stored its water in a huge reservoir the size of a football field. The baths were accessible to all Romans for a minimal fee. Everyone, including poor people, took full advantage of them on a regular basis. Here they would meet friends, exchange local news and gossip, play a game of ball, and get a bath. When bathers entered the bathhouse, they were given a jar of olive oil and a scraper. In the heat of the saunas, they would rub the olive oil all over and scrape their skin clean with the scraper. After the hot sauna and possibly a massage, bathers would finish with a cool dip in a swimming pool.

XII Recycling Latin

Your teacher will now give you time to use your Latin. Think of all you have learned!

- You can say your name!
- You can name the days of the week and the months of the year!
- You can name objects in the classroom!
- You can count and do math!
- You can describe yourself and others and point out parts of the body!
- You can name animals and colors!

When someone asks if you speak Latin: **Dicisne tu Latine?**, now you can answer: **Ita, ego dico Latine!**

Fill in the boxes with the Latin meanings and you will find a mystery word in one of the longest vertical columns. Write the mystery word in Latin and English in the blanks provided:

1. window
2. blue
3. writing tablet
4. tall
5. eye
6. Hello.
7. Wednesday
8. What is it?
9. August
10. bench

_____

_____

Colors: What would this funny monster look like if you could paint the parts of its body? Write the names of the parts of the body and colors you would choose in the blanks below. Then color the parts of the body in the picture:

Part of the body   **Color**

1. _____   _____

2. _____   _____

3. _____   _____

4. _____   _____

5. _____   _____

6. _____   _____

7. _____   _____

8. _____   _____

9. _____   _____

Can you complete these dialogs or express the following ideas in Latin?

1. You overhear the conversation of these two people, who are meeting for the first time. Complete the dialog:

2. Mark is teaching some Latin words to his little brother.
Complete the dialog:

3. What are the colors of
the American flag?

_____   _____   _____

4. What are the names of these parts of the body?

 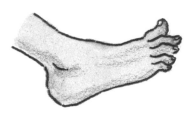 

_____   _____   _____

5. What days of the week are missing from this agenda?

Junius		XII dies Jovis
IX dies Lunae		XIII
X		XIV
XI		XV dies Solis

6. What Latin month is it?

_____ _____ _____

7. Can you name and describe these animals?

_____ _____ _____

_____ _____ _____

Vici is played like Bingo, except that our **Vici** game is played with words. Select Latin words from categories in the vocabulary list on pages 73 to 75 as directed by your teacher. Write one word across in each square at random from the chosen categories.

Your teacher will read the **Vici** words in English. If one of the Latin words on your card matches the English word you hear, mark that square with a small star. When you have five stars in a row, either horizontally, vertically, or diagonally, call out, **"Vici!"** (*"I won!"*)

Vocabulary

Numbers

unus	1
duo	2
tres	3
quattuor	4
quinque	5
sex	6
septem	7
octo	8
novem	9
decem	10
undecim	11
duodecim	12
tredecim	13
quattuordecim	14
quindecim	15
sedecim	16
septendecim	17
duodeviginti	18
undeviginti	19
viginti	20
viginti unus	21
viginti duo	22
viginti tres	23
viginti quattuor	24
viginti quinque	25
viginti sex	26
viginti septem	27
duodetriginta	28
undetriginta	29
triginta	30
triginta unus	31
triginta duo	32
triginta tres	33
triginta quattuor	34
triginta quinque	35
triginta sex	36
triginta septem	37
duodequadraginta	38
undequadraginta	39
quadraginta	40

Days of the week

dies Lunae	Monday
dies Martis	Tuesday
dies Mercurii	Wednesday
dies Jovis	Thursday
dies Veneris	Friday
dies Saturni	Saturday
dies Solis	Sunday

Months of the year

Januarius	January
Februarius	February
Martius	March
Aprilis	April
Maius	May
Junius	June
Julius	July
Augustus	August
September	September
October	October
November	November
December	December

The Classroom

atramentum *n*	ink
calamus *m*	pen
cathedra *f*	teacher's chair
charta *f*	paper
discipula *f*	female student
discipulus *m*	male student
fenestra *f*	window
janua *f*	door
liber *m*	book
magister *m*	male teacher
magistra *f*	female teacher
mensa *f*	table
puella *f*	girl
puer *m*	boy
regula *f*	ruler
stilus *m*	stylus
subsellium *n*	bench
tabula *f*	writing tablet
volumen *n*	scroll

The Body

auris *f*	ear
bracchium *n*	arm
caput *n*	head
crus *n*	leg
manus *f*	hand
nasus *m*	nose
oculus *m*	eye
os *n*	mouth
pes *m*	foot

Adjectives

amicus, amica	lovable, friendly
crassus, crassa	fat
infirmus, infirma	weak
intellegens	intelligent
laetus, laeta	happy
maestus, maesta	sad
malignus, maligna	mean
parvus, parva	short
procerus, procera	tall
pulcher, pulchra	handsome, beautiful
stupidus, stupida	stupid
tenuis	thin
turpis	ugly
validus, valida	strong

Animals

anas *f*	duck
asinus *m*	donkey
avis *f*	bird
canis *m*	dog
equus *m*	horse
feles *f*	cat
gallina *f*	chicken
porcus *m*	pig
pullus *m*	chick
rana *f*	frog
vacca *f*	cow
vulpes *f*	fox

Colors

albus, alba	white
ater, atra	black
caeruleus, caerulea	blue
canus, cana	gray
flavus, flava	yellow
fuscus, fusca	brown
prasinus, prasina	green
rosaceus, rosacea	pink
ruber, rubra	red

Expressions and Phrases

Quod nomen est tibi?	What's your name?
Mihi nomen est . . .	My name is . . .
Et tibi?	And you?
Quid agis?	How are you?
Valeo.	Fine.
Ego quoque valeo.	I'm fine too.
Multas gratias.	Thank you very much.
Salve.	Hello.
Vale.	Good-bye.
Quid novi?	What's new?
Nihil novi.	Nothing's new.
Quot?	How many?
Quid est?	What is it?
Est . . .	It's . . .
Hodie est . . .	Today is . . .
Ego sum . . .	I am . . .
Tu es . . .	You are . . .
Is est . . .	He is . . .
Ea est . . .	She is . . .
Puer est . . .	The boy is . . .
Puella est . . .	The girl is . . .
Cur es . . . ?	Why are you . . . ?
Vici!	I won!
Dicisne tu Latine?	Do you speak Latin?
Ita, ego dico Latine!	Yes, I speak Latin!
Capsula culturae	Culture capsule
Vero.	Yes.
Non.	No.
et	and
nunc	now
quoque	also